YEAR 5

LANGUAGE CONVENTIONS

NAPLAN*-FORMAT PRACTICE TESTS
with answers

Essential preparation for Year 5
NAPLAN* Tests in Language Conventions

DON ROBENS

CORONEOS PUBLICATIONS

YEAR 5 LANGUAGE CONVENTIONS
NAPLAN*-FORMAT PRACTICE TESTS with answers
© Don Robens 2010
Published by Coroneos Publications 2010

ISBN 978-1-921565-44-1

* These tests have been produced by Coroneos Publications independently
  of Australian governments and are not officially endorsed publications of
  the NAPLAN program

THIS BOOK IS AVAILABLE FROM RECOGNISED BOOKSELLERS OR CONTACT:

Coroneos Publications
Telephone: (02) 9624 3977   Facsimile: (02) 9624 3717
Business Address: 6/195 Prospect Highway Seven Hills 2147
Postal Address: PO Box 2 Seven Hills 2147
Website: www. coroneos.com.au or www.basicskillsseries.com
E-mail: coroneospublications@westnet.com.au

Contents

NOTE:

• Students have 40 minutes to complete a test.

• Students must use 2B or HB pencils only.

The spelling mistakes in these sentences have been underlined. Write the correct spelling for each underlined word on the line provided.

1   They were <u>exersising</u>.   1 _____

2   The people were <u>liffting</u> the furniture.   2 _____

3   They were <u>katching</u> a ball.   3 _____

4   They were then <u>bounsing</u> a ball.   4 _____

5   The pencil's <u>lenth</u> was 10 cm.   5 _____

6   They watched the <u>telavision</u>.   6 _____

7   It was a clean <u>enviroment</u>.   7 _____

8   We <u>meesured</u> the lines.   8 _____

Each word is spelled incorrectly.
Write the correct spelling on the lines provided.

9 fotographs _____   **10** varety _____

11 dangeruos _____   **12** microsope _____

Each sentence has one word that is incorrect.
Write the correct spelling of the word on the line provided.

13 The wether was fine.   13 _____

14 The engin was modern.   14 _____

15 Birds have many feethers.   15 _____

16 On the snake's skin were many skales.   16 _____

17 A swimer swam across the pool.   17. _____

**Each sentence has one word that is incorrect.
Write the correct spelling of the word on the line provided.**

18 The mountaines were beautiful.   18 _____

19 The traffic signe said Stop.   19 _____

20 They said goodby.   20 _____

21 That's the smalest fish.   21 _____

22 We drew a spheere.   22 _____

23 It is an enomous property.   23 _____

24 Is this pair of shoes cleen?   24 _____

25 Water is impotant.   25 _____

Read the sentences about *Transport*. The sentences have some gaps. Choose the correct word or words to fill each gap.

Transport

The buses ▨ full.

26
    was   were   is
    ◯   ◯   ◯

Timothy first travelled on a train ▨ caught a bus.

27
    and then   until   when   while
    ◯   ◯   ◯   ◯

Dad helped me find a seat. ▨ sat in a seat.

28
    Now dad   Dad   Then dad
    ◯   ◯   ◯

29 Which sentence has the correct punctuation?

- ⚪ What is the answer.
- ⚪ What is the answer?
- ⚪ What is the, answer?

30 Which sentence has the correct punctuation?

- ⚪ "Whose book is this," asked Tess.
- ⚪ "Whose book is this." asked Tess.
- ⚪ "Whose book is this?" asked Tess.

31 Which word correctly completes the sentence?

The train was full ▆▆▆▆ no more passengers could enter it.

then	so	while	when
⚪	⚪	⚪	⚪

32 Where do the two missing marks ("___") go?

Shade two bubbles

⚪   ⚪ ⚪   ⚪

↓   ↓ ↓   ↓

It's a great day! said the father.

33 Which answer correctly completes the sentence?

Shade one bubble

Ken ▆▆▆▆ some gardening and then helped his dad.

do	does	dug	had done
⚪	⚪	⚪	⚪

34 Which word correctly completes the sentence?

I like ▆▆▆▆ three books.

that	which	these	them
⚪	⚪	⚪	⚪

The sentences below have some gaps.
Choose the correct word or words to fill each gap.

Shade one bubble

There was [ ] much salt on the chips.

35
to   two   too
○   ○   ○

They had [ ] to see the beautiful river.

36
came   come   comes
○   ○   ○

All thought [ ] answers were correct.

37
there   their   they're
○   ○   ○

[ ] all helping.

38
They're   There   Their
○   ○   ○

[ ] reading is wonderful!

39
Your're   Your   You'll
○   ○   ○

Read the sentences about *Computers*. The sentences have some gaps. Choose the correct word or words to fill each gap.

Computers

Shade one bubble

The computer's hum was ▮ than the refrigerator's buzz.

40   quiet   quietest   quieter
               ○   ○   ○

A technician fixed the computer ▮ .

41   quickly   more quickly   quickest
             ○   ○   ○

42 Which word correctly completes the sentence?

The plates were ▮ from the cupboard to use.

       took   take   taken
        ○   ○   ○

43 Which word correctly completes the sentence?

▮ the correct answer?

   Whats   What's   Thats
     ○   ○   ○

44 Which answer correctly completes the sentence?

That is the ▮ plane of the three planes.

    fastest   fast   faster   more faster
      ○   ○   ○   ○

45 **Which word describes how the person walked?**

The person slowly crossed the road.

↑ ↑ ↑
○ ○ ○

Shade one bubble

46 **Which of the following should end with a question mark?**

○ What is the cook's name

○ What we did was not wanted

○ What the lion ate was tasty

○ What we listened to was interesting

47 **Which option correctly completes the sentence?**

Mum cleaned the .

○ floor windows, and kitchen

○ floor; windows and kitchen

○ floor, windows and kitchen

○ floor windows and, kitchen

48 **Which words correctly complete the sentence?**

The performers squinted because .

○ the cameras was flashing

○ the cameras were flashing

○ the cameras is flashing

○ them cameras were flashing

49 Where does the missing comma (,) go?

After the play John waited for a taxi.

50 Which sentence correctly uses the apostrophe (')?

○ Jills' books are over there.

○ Jills book's are over there.

○ Jill's books are over there.

○ Jills books' are over there.

Test 1   **Answers**

1. exercising   2. lifting   3. catching   4. bouncing   5. length   6. television

7. environment   8. measured   9. photographs   10. variety   11. dangerous

12. microscope   13. weather   14. engine   15. feathers   16. scales   17. swimmer

18. mountains 19. sign 20. goodbye 21. smallest 22. sphere 23. enormous

24. clean   25. important   26. were   27. and then   28. Then dad

29. What is the answer?   30. "Whose book is this?" asked Tess.

31. so 32. "It's a great day!" said the father. 33. had done

34. these 35. too 36. come 37. their 38. They're 39. Your

40. quieter 41. quickly 42. taken 43. What's 44. fastest

45. slowly 46. What is the cook's name? 47. floor, windows and kitchen

48. the cameras were flashing 49. ...play, John waited...

50. Jill's books...

The spelling mistakes in these sentences have been underlined. Write the correct spelling for each underlined word on the line provided.

1   They were <u>freindly</u> people.   1 _____

2   Many people were <u>carying</u> chairs.   2 _____

3   Three men were <u>moveing</u> a tree.   3 _____

4   They were then <u>classifing</u> a plant.   4 _____

5   The car's <u>wideth</u> was about 150 cm.   5 _____

6   The vet watched the cat's <u>behavour</u>.   6 _____

7   It was a <u>poisonus</u> snake.   7 _____

8   He <u>combbed</u> his hair.   8 _____

Each word is spelled incorrectly.
Write the correct spelling on the lines provided.

9 filmes _____   **10** orcherds _____

11 soiles _____   **12** powltry _____

Each sentence has one word that is incorrect.
Write the correct spelling of the word on the line provided.

13 The camara was tiny.   13 _____

14 The micrascope was modern.   14 _____

15 The zoo cared for many animels.   15 _____

16 Vegtables were growing.   16 _____

17 The news was heard on the radeo.   17 _____

Each sentence has one word that is incorrect.
Write the correct spelling of the word on the line provided.

18 The picturs were colourful.

18._____

19 The traffic signel turned green.

19 _____

20 It was a good idee.

20 _____

21 That's the bigest fish!

21 _____

22 We drew a sircle.

22 _____

23 It is a coutry property.

23 _____

24 Is this pear of shoes clean?

24 _____

25 We climed the mountain.

25 _____

Read the sentences about *People*. The sentences have some gaps. Choose the correct word or words to fill each gap.

People

Shade one bubble

The man was ▨ taller than his wife.

26   slightly   slight   more slightly

⭘   ⭘   ⭘

Timothy washed his hands before ▨ ate his lunch.

27   he's   his   he   him

⭘   ⭘   ⭘   ⭘

▨ stopped exercising.

28   Immediately, sam   Immediately, Sam   Immediately sam

⭘   ⭘   ⭘

29 **Which sentence has the correct punctuation?**

Shade one bubble

○ Why is that the answer!

○ Why is that the answer?

○ Why is that the answer.

30 **Which sentence has the correct punctuation?**

○ "Whose pen is this?" asked Harry.

○ "Whose pen is this," asked Harry.

○ "Whose pen is this." asked Harry.

31 **Which word correctly completes the sentence?**

The bus was stopped ▨ passengers entered it.

as	after	while	the
○	○	○	○

32 **Where do the two missing marks ("___") go?**

○   ○   ○   ○

Shade two bubbles

↓   ↓   ↓   ↓

Help me please! called the little girl.

33 **Which word correctly completes the sentence?**

Kate ▨ some gardening and then helped her mum.

Shade one bubble

done	does	did	do
○	○	○	○

34 **Which word correctly completes the sentence?**

I like ▨ three colours.

that	this	those	them
○	○	○	○

The sentences below have some gaps.
Choose the correct word or words to fill each gap.

Shade one bubble

_____ many oranges were growing on the tree.

35 To   Two   Too
        ◯   ◯   ◯

We [   ] to the end of the road.

36 come   came   comes
        ◯   ◯   ◯

Everyone thought [   ] answer was correct.

37 there   her   those
        ◯   ◯   ◯

[   ] meals included fruit and vegetables.

38 their   There   Their
        ◯   ◯   ◯

That answer is [   ] done!

39 correct, well   correct. Well   correct well
        ◯   ◯   ◯

Read the sentences about Sounds. The sentences have some gaps. Choose the correct word or words to fill each gap.

Shade one bubble

Sounds

The engine noise was [____] then it should have been.

40   loud   loudest   louder
           ○   ○   ○

A mechanic made the engine [____].

41   quieter   more quiet   quietest
           ○   ○   ○

42 **Which word correctly completes the sentence?**

The milk was [____] from the refrigerator.

       take   taken   took
       ○   ○   ○

43 **Which word correctly completes the sentence?**

[____] the correct answer.

       Thats   That's   Those
       ○   ○   ○

44 **Which answer correctly completes the sentence?**

That is a [____] car than the smaller car.

       fastest   fast   faster   more faster
       ○   ○   ○   ○

45 **Which word describes how the dog ran?**

The dog enthusiastically ran after the ball.

Shade one bubble

46 **Which of the following should end with a question mark?**

○ What is the time

○ What we did was read

○ What the bird ate was a worm

○ What we read was most interesting

47 **Which option correctly completes the sentence?**

Mum used in the cooking.

○ salt pepper and herbs

○ salt, pepper and herbs

○ salt, pepper and herbs,

○ salt, pepper and, herbs

48 **Which words correctly complete the sentence?**

The performer bowed because [   ].

○ the audience were clapping

○ the audience will clap

○ the audience was clapping

○ the audience had clapping

Shade one bubble

49 Where does the missing comma (,) go?

Asking the question carefully Jim then waited for an answer.

⬆   ⬆   ⬆

◯   ◯   ◯

50 Which sentence correctly uses the apostrophe (')?

◯ Jack's books are over there.

◯ Jacks book's are over there.

◯ Jacks books' are over there.

◯ Jacks' books are over there.

Test 2   **Answers**

1. friendly   2. carrying   3. moving   4. classifying   5. width   6. behaviour

7. poisonous   8. combed   9. films   10. orchards   11. soils   12. poultry

13. camera   14. microscope   15. animals   16. vegetables   17. radio

18. pictures   19. signal   20. idea   21. biggest   22. circle   23. country

24. pair   25. climbed   26. slightly   27. he   28. Immediately, Sam

29. Why is that the answer?   30. "Whose pen is this?" asked Harry.

31. while   32. "Help me please!" called the little girl.   33. did

34. those   35. Too   36. came   37. her   38. Their   39. correct. Well

40. louder   41. quieter   42. taken   43. That's   44. faster

45. enthusiastically   46. What is the time?   47. salt, pepper and herbs

48. the audience was clapping   49. …carefully, Jim …

50. Jack's books…

The spelling mistakes in these sentences have been underlined. Write the correct spelling for each underlined word on the line provided.

1   They read the book's <u>titel</u>   1 _____

2   That was a <u>usefull</u> item   2 _____

3   The <u>auther</u> wrote the book   3 _____

4   A writer wrote several <u>storys</u>   4 _____

5   It was an <u>importent</u> story   5 _____

6   Here is an <u>atractive</u> garden   6 _____

7   That's a good <u>ditionary</u>   7 _____

8   In the <u>atlasses</u> were many maps   8 _____

Each word is spelled incorrectly.
Write the correct spelling on the lines provided.

9 churchs _____

10 theaters _____

11 pyramides _____

12 casstles _____

Each sentence has one word that is incorrect.
Write the correct spelling of the word on the line provided.

13 The hospitle was busy.   13 _____

14 The stadeums were modern.   14 _____

15 A king lived in the palase.   15 _____

16 Their experiense was growing.   16 _____

17 They received a good educaton.   17 _____

Each sentence has one word that is incorrect.
Write the correct spelling of the word on the line provided.

18 The opportunites were many.   18 _____

19 There were many choises.   19 _____

20 They learnt worthwhile valuees.   20 _____

21 There are many ocupations.   21 _____

22 We drew a rectangel.   22 _____

23 Emploiment opportunities were there.   23 _____

24 We were leerning about water.   24 _____

25 Over the brigde travelled the traffic.   25 _____

Read the sentences about *Cities*. The sentences have some gaps. Choose the correct word or words to fill each gap.

Cities

Shade one bubble

A city is made up ▨ of modern suburbs.

26   most   mostly   nearly
          ⭕   ⭕   ⭕

William washed his hands before ▨ the snack.

27   ate   eat   eating   eaten
          ⭕   ⭕   ⭕   ⭕

▨ there!

28   Joe. Stop   Joe! Stop   Joe? Stop
          ⭕   ⭕   ⭕

29 Which sentence has the correct punctuation?

⭕ That answer is really clever!

⭕ That answer is very clever.

⭕ That answer is very clever?

30 Which sentence has the correct punctuation?

Shade one bubble

○ "How do I do this?" asked Halley.

○ "How do I do this," asked Halley.

○ "How do I do this." asked Halley.

31 Which word correctly completes the sentence?

_____ the light turned green we drove off.

Then	That	And	When
○	○	○	○

32 Where do the two missing marks ("____") go?

○   ○   ○   ○
↓   ↓   ↓   ↓

Ready, set, go! called the coach.

Shade two bubbles

33 Which answer correctly completes the sentence?

After David _____ his homework he helped his dad.

Shade one bubble

had did	done	had done	is doing
○	○	○	○

34 Which word correctly completes the sentence?

_____ buying a pencil and an exercise book.

I	I've	I'm	Me
○	○	○	○

The sentences below have some gaps.
Choose the correct word or words to fill each gap.

Shade one
bubble

The people walked ▮▮▮ the library.

35   to   two   too

We travelled to ▮▮▮ school for the debate.

36   there   they're   their

Everyone ▮▮▮ the answer was correct.

37   think   thought   through

They went ▮▮▮ the museum.

38   threw   through   though

That fruit is ▮▮▮ delicious!

39   ripe, its   ripe! It's   ripe. Its

Read the sentences about Colours. The sentences have some gaps. Choose the correct word or words to fill each gap.

Colours

That was the _____ of the four colours.

40   best   better   far better

  ◯   ◯   ◯

We had to decide on the colour quite _____.

41   quickest   quickly   quicker

  ◯   ◯   ◯

42 **Which word correctly completes the sentence?**

The car was ▨ we had parked it.

wear   were   where

◯   ◯   ◯

Shade one bubble

43 **Which word correctly completes the sentence?**

▨ the correct way to go.

Its   It   It's

◯   ◯   ◯

44 **Which answer correctly completes the sentence?**

That is the ▨ of the two elephants.

larger   largest   large   more larger

◯   ◯   ◯   ◯

45 **Which word describes how the elephant moved?**

The elephant powerfully moved across the ground.

↑   ↑   ↑

◯   ◯   ◯

46 **Which of the following should end with a question mark?**

◯ They are all right

◯ Are they all right

◯ All right – wonderful

◯ They're all right

47 **Which option correctly completes the sentence?**

○ The nurse used ▢ .

○ bandages water and powder

○ bandages, water and powder?

○ bandages, water and powder.

○ bandages, water and powder

48 **Which words correctly complete the sentence?**

The pencils ▢ .

○ was in the pencil case.

○ were in the pencil case.

○ is in the pencil case.

○ am in the pencil case.

49 **Where does the missing comma (,) go?**

After jumping over the path Michael sat on a seat.

↑   ↑   ↑
○   ○   ○

50 **Which sentence correctly uses the apostrophe (')?**

○ These were Georges book's.

○ These were Georges books'.

○ These were George's books.

○ These were Georges' books.

Test 3	**Answers**

1. title 2. useful 3. author 4. stories 5. important 6. attractive

7. dictionary 8. atlases 9. churches 10. theatres 11. pyramids 12. castles

13. hospital 14. stadiums 15. palace 16. experience 17. education

18. opportunities 19. choices 20. values 21. occupations 22. rectangle

23. Employment 24. learning 25. bridge 26. mostly 27. eating

28. Joe! Stop 29. That answer is really clever!

30. "How do I do this?" asked Halley. 31. When

32. "Ready, set, go!" called the coach. 33. had done 34. I'm 35. to

36. their 37. thought 38. through 39. ripe! It's 40. best 41. quickly

42. where 43. It's 44. larger 45. powerfully 46. Are they all right

47. bandages, water and powder 48. were in the pencil case

49. ...path, Michael... 50. These were George's books.

The spelling mistakes in these sentences have been underlined. Write the correct spelling for each underlined word on the line provided.

1 The book's cover was <u>shiney</u>.

1 _____

2 That is a <u>beutiful</u> painting.

2 _____

3 The vegetation was <u>nateral</u>.

3 _____

4 The writer is <u>arrangeing</u> it.

4 _____

5 It was an <u>importent</u> book.

5 _____

6 There is an amazing <u>reinbow</u>.

6 _____

7 It was an <u>ugli</u> scene.

7 _____

8 We looked <u>though</u> the telescope.

8 _____

Each word is spelled incorrectly.
Write the correct spelling on the lines provided.

9   thoughful_____   10   filum _____

11   languege _____   12   listuning _____

Each sentence has one word that is incorrect.
Write the correct spelling of the word on the line provided.

13   The computer user used the intenet.   13 _____

14   It was a modern keybord.   14 _____

15   A man used the computer programe.   15 _____

16   A viris was in the computer.   16 _____

17   He had a wonderful memary.   17 _____

Each sentence has one word that is incorrect.
Write the correct spelling of the word on the line provided.

18 The equipement was expensive.   18 _____

19 That is the controll tower.   19 _____

20 There were circuites in the computer.   20 _____

21 There are many ocupations.   21 _____

22 Conect the wires here.   22 _____

23 Editeing is important in writing.   23 _____

24 That is a colunm graph.   24 _____

25 We veiwed the photos.   25 _____

These sentences have gaps.
Choose the correct word or words to fill each gap.

Shade one bubble

[   ] is an important subject.

26   Engliss   English   english
              ○   ○   ○

Before [   ] start they'll practise questions.

27   they'l   their   they   they're
              ○   ○   ○   ○

[   ] at this!

28   Gina. Look   Gina! Look   Gina, Look
              ○   ○   ○

29 Which sentence has the correct punctuation?

That work is wonderful?

That work is wonderful

That work is wonderful!

30 Which sentence has the correct punctuation?

Mark called out, "The tap is dripping?"

Mark called out, "The tap is dripping!"

Mark called out, "The tap is dripping."

31 Which answer correctly completes the sentence?

Dad, mum and their children [   ].

      is going   are going   going   gone
        ○   ○   ○   ○

32 **Where do the two missing marks (" ___ ") go?**

Shade two bubbles

○   ○   ○   ○
↓   ↓   ↓   ↓
Are you ready to leave? called mum.

33 **Which word correctly completes the sentence?**

Shade one bubble

The cat sat ▮▮▮ the window sill.

in   at   on   of

○   ○   ○   ○

34 **Which word correctly completes the sentence?**

▮▮▮ going to the zoo.

We   We've   We're   Where

○   ○   ○   ○

The sentences below have some gaps.
Choose the correct word or words to fill each gap.

Shade one bubble

The people ▮ walking to the library.

35   is   are   was
           ○   ○   ○

Warren was ▮ up early.

36   waken   woke   woken
           ○   ○   ○

It was an ▮ tree.

37   huge   enormous   beautiful
           ○   ○   ○

They travelled ▮ the railway tunnel.

38   throw   through   threw
           ○   ○   ○

Those clothes are ▮ need washing!

39   dirty, they   dirty! They   dirty? They
           ○   ○   ○

Read the sentences about Learning. The sentences have some gaps. Choose the correct word or words to fill each gap.

Learning

Shade one bubble

That was the ▮ of the three computers.

40   most modern   more modern   modernist
            ○   ○   ○

Jim insisted ▮ he was right.

41   that   of that   over that   in that
           ○   ○   ○   ○

42 Which word correctly completes the sentence?

▮ ready! Let's go!

W're   We're   Where
  ○   ○   ○

43 Which word correctly completes the sentence?

▮ the street we want.

There're   Theres'   There's
   ○   ○   ○

44 Which answer correctly completes the sentence?

This is the ▮ of the eight insects.

tinier   tiniest   most tiny   more tiny
  ○   ○   ○   ○

45 **Which word describes how the eagle glided?**

Shade one bubble

The eagle gracefully glided across the sky.

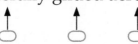

46 **Which of the following should end with an exclamation mark?**

- ⬭ The nest was small
- ⬭ A nest was in the tree
- ⬭ Can you see the nest
- ⬭ There's the nest

47 **Which option correctly completes the sentence?**

The car needed .

- ⬭ water, petrol oil and air.
- ⬭ water, petrol, oil and air?
- ⬭ water, petrol, oil and air.
- ⬭ water; petrol, oil and air.

48 **Which words correctly complete the sentence?**

The chair � .

- ⬭ were in the library.
- ⬭ was in the library.
- ⬭ are in the library.
- ⬭ there in the library.

49 **Where does the missing comma (,) go?**

The plane landed at Sydney Melbourne and Adelaide.

           ⬆   ⬆   ⬆

           ◯   ◯   ◯

50 **Which sentence correctly uses the apostrophe (')?**

- ◯ Have you seen Peters book?
- ◯ Have you seen Peters' book?
- ◯ Have you seen Peter's book?
- ◯ Have you seen Pete'rs book?

Year 5 Language Conventions
NAPLAN* Format Practice Tests

Test 4   **Answers**

1. shiny **2.** beautiful **3.** natural **4.** arranging **5.** important **6.** rainbow

7. ugly **8.** through **9.** thoughtful **10.** film **11.** language **12.** listening

13. internet **14.** keyboard **15.** program **16.** virus **17.** memory

18. equipment **19.** control **20.** circuits **21.** occupations **22.** Connect

23. Editing **24.** column **25.** viewed **26.** English **27.** they

28. Gina! Look **29.** That work is wonderful!

30. Mark called out, "The tap is dripping!". **31.** are going

32. "Are you ready to leave?" called mum. **33.** on **34.** We're **35.** are

36. woken **37.** enormous **38.** through **39.** dirty! They

40. most modern **41.** that **42.** We're **43.** There's **44.** tiniest

45. gracefully **46.** There's the nest **47.** water, petrol, oil and air.

48. was in the library. **49.** …Sydney, Melbourne…

50. Have you seen Peter's book?

The spelling mistakes in these sentences have been underlined. Write the correct spelling for each underlined word on the line provided.

1 They were <u>practicing</u> for the test.   1 _____

2 <u>Sceince</u> is interesting.   2 _____

3 The <u>diagrame</u> is clear.   3 _____

4 The <u>studants</u> loved the test.   4 _____

5 The <u>musik</u> was soothing.   5 _____

6 They entered the <u>libary</u>.   6 _____

7 It was a large <u>televison</u>.   7 _____

8 It was an interesting <u>ilustration</u>.   8 _____

Each word is spelled incorrectly.
Write the correct spelling on the lines provided.

9 qestions _____ **10** modurn _____

11 guideing _____ **12** meesuring _____

Each sentence has one word that is incorrect.
Write the correct spelling of the word on the line provided.

13 Unkle Harry was here. 13 _____

14 The aurnt was kind. 14 _____

15 The childern were hungry. 15 _____

16 Their parants were busy. 16 _____

17 The adultes paid full fare. 17 _____

Each sentence has one word that is incorrect.
Write the correct spelling of the word on the line provided.

18 All the familes were there.   18 _____

19 The wifes were thoughtful.   19 _____

20 The cousines met.   20 _____

21 The yungest person was seven.   21 _____

22 The peeple enjoyed the day.   22 _____

23 They studied their ancesters.   23 _____

24 In the cupboardes were many books.   24 _____.

25 The windowes were closed.   25 _____

These sentences have gaps.
Choose the correct word or words to fill each gap.

Shade one bubble

26 ▨ Maths an important subject?

Aren't   Is'nt   Isn't
○   ○   ○

27 Before midday ▨ hoping to be there.

where   wer'e   we're   there're
○   ○   ○   ○

28 Hey ▨ at this fascinating creature!

Barry! Look   Barry, look   Barry. Look
○   ○   ○

29 Which sentence has the correct punctuation?

○ Is today Tuesday.

○ Is today, Tuesday.

○ Is today Tuesday?

30 Which sentence has the correct punctuation?

○ "I've caught a fish!" yelled Chris.

○ "I've caught a fish?" yelled Chris.

○ "I've caught a fish," yelled Chris.

31 Which answer correctly completes the sentence?

The family_____ for a walk.

has going   were gone   has gone   is gone
○   ○   ○

32 Where do the two missing marks (" ___ ") go?

○   ○   ○   ○
↓   ↓   ↓   ↓

That's the answer, replied Robert.

Shade two bubbles

33 Which word correctly completes the sentence?

The coin fell ▉ the drain.

Shade one bubble

on	to	into	over
○	○	○	○

34 Which word correctly completes the sentence?

That is what ▉ been wanting to see.

we	we've	wev'e	we're
○	○	○	○

The sentences below have some gaps.
Choose the correct word or words to fill each gap.

Shade one bubble

The crowd ▮▮▮ watching the game.

35   were   was   am
         ○   ○   ○

The bottle was ▮▮▮ up.

36   shook   shake   shaken
         ○   ○   ○

It was an ▮▮▮ book.

37   small   wonderful   interesting
         ○   ○   ○

I had ▮▮▮ the ball at the target.

38   threw   through   thrown
         ○   ○   ○

The car is ▮▮▮ needs cleaning!

39   dirty, it   dirty. it   dirty! It
         ○   ○   ○

Read the sentences about Homes. The sentences have some gaps. Choose the correct word or words to fill each gap.

Homes

Shade one bubble

That home was in the [ ] of the three suburbs.

40   newest   newer   new
            ○   ○   ○

Ken insisted [ ] replying to the letter.

41   in   as   to   at
            ○   ○   ○   ○

42 Which word correctly completes the sentence?

They had [ ] at the shopping centre.

      meet   meat   met
       ○   ○   ○

43 Which word correctly completes the sentence?

[ ] our friends.

      There're   Theres'   There's
        ○   ○   ○

44 Which answer correctly completes the sentence?

This is the [ ] of the ten paintings.

   most value   more valuable   most valuable
       ○   ○   ○

45 **Which word describes how the tree swayed?**

Shade one bubble

The tree slowly swayed in the breeze.

---

46 **Which of the following should end with an exclamation mark?**

○ Can I help you

○ Can I help

○ Help

○ Why

---

47 **Which option correctly completes the sentence?**

The student read a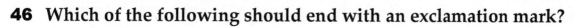

○ newspaper a computer screen and a book.

○ newspaper, a computer screen and a book.

○ newspaper, a computer screen and a book?

○ newspaper, a computer, screen and a book.

---

48 **Which words correctly complete the sentence?**

The dog ▮▮▮ .

○ are alone at home.

○ is alone at home.

○ am alone at home.

○ were alone at home.

49 **Where does the missing comma (,) go?**

We travelled by car, train bus and ferry.

⬆   ⬆   ⬆

◯   ◯   ◯

50 **Which sentence correctly uses the apostrophe (')?**

◯ That is the schools' property.

◯ That is the schools property'.

◯ That' is the schools property.

◯ That is the school's property.

Test 5   **Answers**

1. practising 2. Science 3. diagram 4. students 5. music 6. library

7. television 8. illustration 9. questions 10. modern 11. guiding

12. measuring 13. Uncle 14. aunt 15. children 16. parents 17. adults

18. families 19. wives 20. cousins 21. youngest 22. people

23. ancestors 24. cupboards 25. windows 26. Isn't 27. we're

28. Barry! Look 29. Is today Tuesday?

30. "I've caught a fish!" yelled Chris. 31. has gone

32. "That's the answer," replied Robert. 33. into 34. we've

35. was 36. shaken 37. interesting 38. thrown 39. dirty! It

40. newest 41. in 42. met 43. There're 44. most valuable

45. slowly 46. Help 47. newspaper, a computer screen and a book.

48. is alone at home. 49. …train, bus…

50. That is the school's property.

The spelling mistakes in these sentences have been underlined. Write the correct spelling for each underlined word on the line provided.

1   The floore was clean   1 _____

2   In the gardan were several fruit trees   2 _____

3   The seilings of the rooms were high   3 _____

4   The astronomers used a teliscope   4 _____

5   Lightes lit up the darkness   5 _____

6   People sat on chaires   6 _____

7   The coin was spining   7 _____

8   The catarpiller was growing bigger   8 _____

Each word is spelled incorrectly.
Write the correct spelling on the lines provided.

9 climbeing _____   **10** milions _____

11 thoosands _____   **12** tasteing _____

Each sentence has one word that is incorrect.
Write the correct spelling of the word on the line provided.

13 It was a beatiful butterfly.   13 _____

14 He was chooing the apple.   14 _____

15 The can was emptied of pettrol.   15 _____

16 The wheal on the car was wobbling.   16 _____

17 Electrcity was needed.   17 _____

Each sentence has one word that is incorrect.
Write the correct spelling of the word on the line provided.

18 He looked through the mikroscope.   18 _____

19 It matchs the room colour.   19 _____

20 The helecopter flew overhead.   20 _____

21 They used compases.   21 _____

22 Fuele was needed to make fire burn.   22 _____

23 They studied the wepons.   23 _____

24 The car travelled three kilameters.   24 _____

25 Its lenght was eight centimetres.   25 _____

These sentences have gaps.
Choose the correct word or words to fill each gap.

Shade one bubble

26 Why ▢ the tree's leaves growing?

wasn't   isn't   weren't
   ○   ○   ○

27 Why ▢ the door been closed?

has'nt   have'nt   hasn't   haven't
   ○   ○   ○   ○

28 Oh ▢ already ten o'clock!

dear! Its   dear! It's   dear? It's
   ○   ○   ○

29 Which sentence has the correct punctuation?

○ Today's the day

○ Today's the day?

○ Today's the day!

30 Which sentence has the correct punctuation?

○ "I'm finished!" called Kate.

○ "I'm finished;" called Kate.

○ "I'm finished?" called Kate.

31 Which answer correctly completes the sentence?

The chickens ▢ in the garden.

is there   were there   am there   was there
   ○   ○   ○   ○

32 **Where do the two missing marks (" ___ ") go?**

Shade two bubbles

Did you like the book? asked Dad.

33 **Which word correctly completes the sentence?**

The dog ran after the ball ▇▇ .

Shade one bubble

   too   to   two   toe

   ◯   ◯   ◯   ◯

34 **Which word correctly completes the sentence?**

They ▇▇ home.

   is   wasn't   isn't   weren't

   ◯   ◯   ◯   ◯

The sentences below have some gaps.
Choose the correct word or words to fill each gap.

Shade one bubble

The audience ▨ watching the actors on the stage.

35

was	were	am
○	○	○

The author ▨ worked for eight hours.

36

is	have	has
○	○	○

It was a ▨ movie.

37

inspiring	clever	interesting
○	○	○

I ▨ the ball hit the target.

38

saw	seen	had sawn
○	○	○

The oven is ▨ careful!

39

hot, be	hot? Be	hot! Be
○	○	○

Read the sentences about Measuring. The sentences have some gaps. Choose the correct word or words to fill each gap.

Shade one bubble

Measuring

The land was ▉ carefully.

40   measures   measuring   measured
              ○   ○   ○

Everyone ▉ the room enjoyed themselves.

41   into   over   a   in
            ○   ○   ○   ○

42 Which answer correctly completes the sentence?

They ▉ to consider the data.

had meet   have meet   met
   ○   ○   ○

43 Which word correctly completes the sentence?

▉ measuring the timber.

Their're   They're   There're
   ○   ○   ○

44 Which answer correctly completes the sentence?

This is the ▉ of the two rooms.

most used   more used   more using
   ○   ○   ○

45 **Which word describes how the wind blew?**

The wind blew fiercely through the trees.

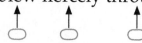

46 **Which of the following should end with a question mark?**

○ I know the answer

○ That answer is correct

○ That's the answer

○ What's the answer

47 **Which option correctly completes the sentence?**

They looked at

○ a white blue, red and silver car.

○ a white, blue red and silver car.

○ a white, blue, red and silver car.

○ a white, blue red and, silver car.

48 **Which words correctly complete the sentence?**

During the test they .

○ was busy.

○ were busy.

○ were most busier.

○ were more busier.

49 Where does the missing comma (,) go?

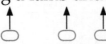

Shade one bubble

They saw a dog a lamb and a horse.
          ↑   ↑   ↑
         ○   ○   ○

50 Which sentence correctly uses the apostrophe (')?

  ○ Is' that the ladys phone?

  ○ Is that the ladys phone'?

  ○ Is that the lady's phone?

  ○ Is that the ladys' phone?

Test 6   **Answers**

1. floor 2. garden 3. ceilings 4. telescope 5. Lights 6. chairs

7. spinning 8. caterpillar 9. climbing 10. millions 11. thousands

12. tasting 13. beautiful 14. chewing 15. petrol 16. wheel 17. Electricity

18. microscope 19. matches 20. helicopter 21. compasses 22. Fuel

23. weapons 24. kilometres 25. length 26. weren't 27. hasn't

28. dear! It's 29. Today's the day!

30. "I'm finished!" called Kate. 31. were there

32. "Did you like the book?" asked Dad. 33. too 34. weren't

35. was 36. has 37. clever 38. saw 39. hot! Be

40. measured 41. in 42. met 43. They're 44. more used

45. fiercely 46. What's the answer 47. a white, blue, red and silver car.

48. were busy. 49. …a dog, a lamb…

50. Is that the lady's phone?

The spelling mistakes in these sentences have been underlined. Write the correct spelling for each underlined word on the line provided.

1   The tree was seven <u>meters</u> tall

1_____

2   The bucket had ten <u>liters</u> of water in it

2_____

3   The water was <u>boyling</u>

3_____

4   A <u>thermometre</u> measured the temperature

4_____

5   A <u>docter</u> knew the answer

5_____

6   <u>Engineres</u> worked hard

6_____

7   The coin was <u>spining</u>

7_____

8   The <u>biulder</u> worked on the home

8_____

Each word is spelled incorrectly.
Write the correct spelling on the lines provided.

9 haert _____   **10** mucsles _____

11 stomech _____   **12** forhead _____

Each sentence has one word that is incorrect.
Write the correct spelling of the word on the line provided.

13 A bird's skelaton was in the museum   13 _____

14 They studied the diseeses   14 _____

15 Veines took blood back to the heart   15 _____

16 Echoss were heard   16 _____

17 The audience was claping.   17 _____

Each sentence has one word that is incorrect.
Write the correct spelling of the word on the line provided.

18 The cicadas were druming loudly

18 _____

19 It matchs the car style

19 _____

20 They finished the quizes

20 _____

21 Radio statons spread the news

21 _____

22 They swam during the morneing

22 _____

23 April was the fourth moonth

23 _____

24 Many vehickles crossed the bridge

24 _____

25 The yaeht was sailing on the harbour

25 _____

These sentences have gaps.
Choose the correct word or words to fill each gap.

Shade one bubble

We ▢ the heavy boxes.

26 were carried   has carried   had carried
          ○   ○   ○

We ▢ the test.

27   has done   have did   have done
            ○   ○   ○

▢ ready!

28 Mum! Im   Mum! i'm   Mum! I'm
          ○   ○   ○

29 Which sentence has the correct punctuation?

○ Its Tuesday.

○ Its' Tuesday isn't it!

○ It's Tuesday isn't it?

30 Which sentence has the correct punctuation?

○ "That's first," yelled William.

○ "That's first!" yelled William.

○ "That's first." yelled William.

31 Which answer correctly completes the sentence?

They ▢ there.

   was over   were over   am over   is over
      ○   ○   ○   ○

32 Where do the two missing marks (" ____ ") go?

Shade two bubbles

What is the time now? asked Tom.

33 Which word correctly completes the sentence?

Shade one bubble

Each person read [   ] answer to check it.

there're	there	their	they're
◯	◯	◯	◯

34 Which word correctly completes the sentence?

She [   ] the answer.

no	new	knew	known
◯	◯	◯	◯

The sentences below have some gaps.
Choose the correct word or words to fill each gap.

Shade one bubble

The dogs [   ] waiting for something to eat.

35   was   is   were
            ○   ○   ○

[   ] you feel hungry yet?

36   Does   Did   Do   Are
           ○   ○   ○   ○

It was an [   ] garden.

37   relaxing   beautiful   unusual
           ○   ○   ○

[   ] attending the function.

38   I've   I'm   I
           ○   ○   ○

That meal is [   ] I have some more?

39 ○ delicious, may

       ○ delicious! May

       ○ delicious? May

Read the sentences about Weather. The sentences have some gaps. Choose the correct word or words to fill each gap.

Weather

Shade one bubble

The temperature ▓ risen.

40   had slower   has slowly   slowly
              ○   ○   ○

Everybody ▓ the room.

41   has enter   entering   is entered   has entered
           ○   ○   ○   ○

42 Which answer correctly completes the sentence?

▓ those the correct answers?

       Are'nt   Isn't   Are
        ○   ○   ○

43 Which word correctly completes the sentence?

▓ waiting for the library to open.

      We're   There're   Their
       ○   ○   ○

44 Which answer correctly completes the sentence?

This is the ▓ of the five colours.

   most liked   more liked   liked
      ○   ○   ○

45 **Which word describes how the rain fell?**

The rain fell heavily to the ground.

46 **Which of the following should end with a question mark?**

○ What's the date

○ It's the first day of March

○ That's the date

○ Here's the date

47 **Which option correctly completes the sentence?**

Mr Brown bought

○ a blue, white, red and striped, shirt.

○ a blue, white red, and striped shirt.

○ a blue, white, red and striped shirt.

○ a blue white, red and, striped shirt.

48 **Which words correctly complete the sentence?**

During the afternoon they .

○ saw the snake.

○ seen the snake.

○ had saw the snake.

○ are seen the snake.

49 Where does the missing comma (,) go?

Jane saw a lizard an eagle and a crow.

50 Which sentence correctly uses the apostrophe (')?

○ Have you' checked Sams answers?

○ Have you checked Sam's answers?

○ Have you checked Sams' answers?

○ Have you checked Sams answers'?

© Don Robens
Coroneos Publications

Year 5 Language Conventions
NAPLAN* Format Practice Tests

Test 7   **Answers**

1. metres **2.** litres **3.** boiling **4.** thermometer **5.** doctor **6.** Engineers

7. spinning **8.** builder **9.** heart **10.** muscles **11.** stomach

12. forehead **13.** skeleton **14.** diseases **15.** Veins **16.** Echoes **17.** clapping

18. drumming **19.** matches **20.** quizzes **21.** stations **22.** morning

23. month **24.** vehicles **25.** yacht **26.** had carried **27.** have done

28. Mum! I'm **29.** It's Tuesday isn't it?

30. "That's first!" yelled William. **31.** were over

32. "What is the time now?" asked Tom. **33.** their **34.** knew

35. were **36.** Do **37.** unusual **38.** I'm **39.** delicious! May

40. has slowly **41.** has entered **42.** Are **43.** We're **44.** most liked

45. heavily **46.** What's the date **47.** a blue, white, red and striped shirt.

48. saw the snake. **49.** …a lizard, an eagle…

50. Have you checked Sam's answers?